2022 CALIFORNIA DRIVER'S PERMIT PRACTICE TEST

CA DMV WRITTEN TEST QUESTIONS AND EXPLANATIONS

BRYAN HOLLOWAY

D1707286

PRACTICE TEST

This practice test was designed to simulate the California DMV written test which has 46 questions. In order to pass, you must answer 38 questions correctly.

The more times you review these questions and explanations, the more you'll improve your chances of passing the California written test to get your learner's permit and driver's license.

Find additional study guides and online driving courses on our website at *www.DMVstudy.com*.

Question 1: If a school bus stops ahead of you and turns on its flashing red lights, you are legally required to:

A. Stop and wait until the lights stop flashing before continuing to drive.

B. Pass the bus on the left.

C. Go around the bus on the right if you have enough room.

The correct answer is A. If a school bus stops ahead of you and turns on its flashing red lights, you are legally required to stop and wait until the lights stop flashing before you continue to drive.

Question 2: If a police car turns on its siren behind you, you should:

A. Continue driving until you reach a public parking lot.

B. Stop immediately in the middle of the road.

C. Turn on your right turn signal and look for a safe place to pull over.

The correct answer is C. If a police car turns on its siren behind you, you should turn on your right turn signal to let the officer know that you see them and intend to stop.

Then, look for a safe place to pull over.

Question 3: If you are issued a traffic citation, you must:

A. Appear in court or pay a fine.

B. Make excuses or cry to get out of the ticket.

C. Offer money to the officer in exchange for canceling the ticket.

The correct answer is A. If you are issued a traffic citation, you must appear in court if you wish to dispute it or pay a fine.

Question 4: If you are involved in a "fender bender" or minor collision:

A. You don't need to stop if no one appears injured.

B. You must stop and exchange information with the other driver.

C. You don't need to stop if you hit a parked car with no passengers inside.

The correct answer is B. Even if you are involved in a minor collision, you must still stop to check on the other driver and exchange information.

Question 5: In California, traffic violations stay on your driving record for at least _____.

A. 12 months

B. 24 months

C. 36 months

The correct answer is C. In California, traffic violations stay on your driving record for at least 36 months.

Question 6: You are required by law to _____ when entering a road construction zone in California.

A. Honk the horn.

B. Turn on your low-beam headlights.

C. Turn on your high-beam headlights.

The correct answer is B. You are required by law to turn on your low-beam headlights when you enter a road construction zone in California.

Question 7: It is illegal for anyone to operate a vehicle in California if their blood alcohol level (BAC) is _____ or higher.

A. 0.08%

B. 0.05%

C. 0.03%

The correct answer is A. In California, the legal limit is a BAC of 0.08%.

Question 8: California's Basic Speed Limit Law says:

A. You should always drive the posted speed limit.

B. You should never drive faster than is safe for conditions.

C. It is okay to drive faster than the posted speed limit to keep up with traffic flow.

The correct answer is B. California's Basic Speed Limit Law says that you should never drive faster than is safe for conditions.

Question 9: Which of the following increases your chances of being involved in a crash?

A. Looking at your phone.

B. Driving when you are tired.

C. Both A and B.

The correct answer is C. Driving while you are tired or looking at your phone can increase your odds of getting into an accident.

Question 10. How often should you check your tire pressure?

A. Every three months.

B. At least once a month or before a long road trip.

C. Every six months.

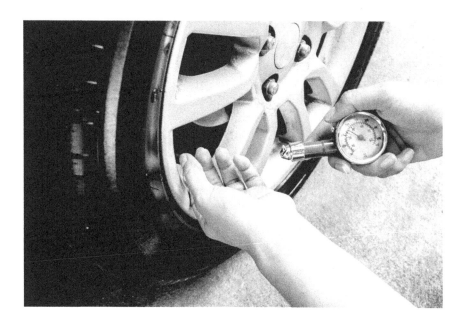

The correct answer is B. You should check your tire pressure at least once a month or before going on a long car trip.

Question 11: Unless otherwise posted, the speed limit in a school zone is:

A. 55 mph

B. 25 mph

C. 5 mph

The correct answer is B. Unless otherwise posted, the speed limit in an active school zone is 25 mph.

Question 12: *Managing space* **is a defensive driving skill that involves:**

A. Understanding the meaning of road signs and signals.

B. Leaving enough room between you and the car in front of you or to the sides of you.

C. Knowing when to turn on your headlights.

The correct answer is B. *"Managing space"* is a defensive driving skill that involves leaving enough room between you and the car in front of you or to the sides of your vehicle.

Question 13: One important fact to know about large trucks is:

A. They take longer to stop than smaller passenger vehicles.

B. They can speed up quickly.

C. They can stop more quickly than smaller cars.

The correct answer is A. It is important to know that it takes large trucks longer to stop than smaller passenger vehicles.

If you slow down or stop quickly in front of a large truck, it could cause a collision.

Question 14: If you are driving after sunset or before sunrise, you must:

A. Turn on your windshield wipers.

B. Turn on your low-beam headlights.

C. Turn on your fog lights.

The correct answer is B. If you are driving after sunset or before sunrise, you must turn on your low-beam headlights.

Question 15: A traffic signal with a steady red light means:

A. You may turn left if there is no oncoming traffic.

B. You must stop at the white line or before the intersection if no line is present.

C. You must yield to oncoming traffic, but you do not have to stop if no one is coming.

The correct answer is B. If you come to a traffic signal with a steady red light, you must stop at the white line or before entering the intersection and wait until the light changes to green before proceeding.

Question 16: When are you required to wear a seat belt?

A. Any time you are driving faster than 25 mph.

B. Any time you are driving at any speed.

C. Only when driving on multi-lane highways.

The correct answer is B. Seatbelts are the law. Therefore, you (and your passengers) must wear a seatbelt anytime you are driving.

Question 17: Why is it important to adjust the driver's seat?

A. To make sure you'll be comfortable.

B. To be able to reach the pedals and see clearly out the windshield.

C. So that the person sitting behind you has enough legroom.

The correct answer is B. It is important to adjust your seat to reach the pedals and see clearly out the windshield easily.

Question 18: The speed limit when driving through a blind intersection (with no stop sign or signal) is:

A. 45 mph

B. 30 mph

C. 15 mph

The correct answer is C. The speed limit when driving through a blind intersection is 15 mph.

Question 19: When driving, you should:

A. Fix your gaze on the center of the road immediately in front of you.

B. Constantly scan your surroundings for situations that could cause an accident.

C. Focus only on the car in front of you.

The correct answer is B. When you are driving, constantly scan your surroundings for potential dangers.

This includes looking ahead 10-15 seconds, looking to the sides of your car, and checking your mirrors often to see what's going on around you.

Question 20: A safe following distance in good driving conditions is:

A. 1 second

B. 2 seconds

C. 4 seconds

The correct answer is C. A safe following distance in good driving conditions is 4 seconds.

Remember to allow more space when the road or weather conditions are not ideal.

Question 21: When you come to an intersection, you should look:

A. Right, left, then right again before crossing.

B. Left, right, then left again before crossing.

C. Straight ahead if you have a green light.

The correct answer is B. When you come to an intersection, you should look left, right, and then back to your left again before crossing since traffic coming from the left will be closest to you.

Remember, just because you have a green light or the right-of-way does not mean that other drivers will always comply. They might be distracted or driving under the influence.

Question 22: A blind spot is:

A. An area of the road that is difficult to see because it is too far ahead of you.

B. A special crosswalk for blind pedestrians.

C. The area around a vehicle that a driver can't see in their rearview or side mirrors.

The correct answer is C. A blind spot is an area around a vehicle that a driver can't see in their rearview or side mirrors.

Question 23: If you are driving 55 mph, how much space will you need to come to a complete stop?

A. 100 feet

B. 250 feet

C. 400 feet

The correct answer is C. If you are going 55 mph, you will need 400 feet of space to come to a complete stop.

Question 24: When a long vehicle, such as a tractor-trailer, makes a turn, the back wheels have a _____ path than those in the front.

A. Longer.

B. Shorter.

C. The same length.

The correct answer is B. When long vehicles make turns, the back wheels have a shorter path than those in the front.

This causes them to have to swing out wide when turning.

Question 25: It is against the law to leave your high-beam headlights on when:

A. You are driving in the daytime.

B. You are approaching another vehicle.

C. You are driving on a rural road.

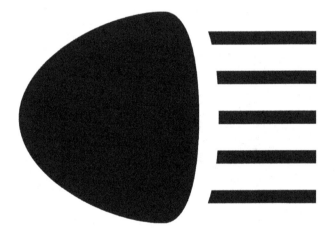

The correct answer is B. It is against the law to leave your high-beam headlights on when you are approaching another vehicle.

Question 26: It is illegal for any person under the age of 21 to drive a car if their blood alcohol level (BAC) is greater than _____.

A. 0.08%

B. 0.01%

C. 0.04%

The correct answer is B. According to California's *"no tolerance policy,"* it is illegal for anyone under 21 to drive if their BAC is greater than 0.01.

Question 27: You can reduce the risk of carbon monoxide poisoning by:

A. Never running the engine in a garage with the door closed.

B. Opening your car windows with you are parked outside with the engine running.

C. Both A and B.

The correct answer is C. You can reduce the risk of carbon monoxide poisoning by not running the engine in a garage when the door is closed and opening your car windows with you are parked outside with the engine running.

You should also have your exhaust system checked regularly for leaks.

Question 28: The speed limit when driving near or crossing railroad tracks is _____ unless otherwise posted.

A. 5 mph

B. 10 mph

C. 15 mph

The correct answer is C. Unless otherwise posted, the speed limit when driving near or crossing railroad tracks is 15 mph.

Question 29: When driving in poor weather conditions:

A. It takes longer to react and stop.

B. It takes the same amount of time to react and stop.

C. It takes less time to react and stop.

The correct answer is A. For example, when driving in poor weather conditions such as rain or fog, it takes longer to stop than when operating in perfect conditions.

Question 30: When entering or merging onto the freeway, you should drive:

A. At or near the same speed as the flow of traffic.

B. 25 mph slower than the flow of traffic.

C. Faster than the flow of traffic.

The correct answer is A. When entering the freeway, you should drive at or near the same speed as traffic flow.

Going significantly faster or slower than the flow of traffic can increase your chances of causing a crash.

Question 31: If you come to a safety zone where people are boarding or exiting a bus or trolley, you must:

A. Drive through the safety zone at no more than 40 mph.

B. Stop and wait until all pedestrians are safely away from the road before you proceed.

C. Honk your horn as you drive through to let pedestrians know that they should wait to cross.

The correct answer is B. If you come to a safety zone where people are boarding or exiting a bus or trolley, you must stop and wait until all pedestrians are safely away from the road before you proceed.

Question 32: Which type of vehicle must AL-WAYS stop before crossing train tracks?

A. School or city busses.

B. Truck that transport hazardous materials.

C. Both A and B.

The correct answer is C. Both busses and trucks transporting hazardous materials must always stop before crossing railroad tracks, regardless of whether there is a stop sign or signal.

Question 33: You should stop at least _____ feet from the nearest railroad tracks when crossing devices such as lights are active or blinking.

A. 15

B. 10

C. 5

The correct answer is A. You should stop at least 15 feet from (but no more than 50 feet) from the nearest railroad tracks when crossing devices, such as lights, are active or blinking.

Question 34: If an emergency vehicle such as an ambulance, fire truck, or police car, is using its siren and lights, you must:

A. Pull over and stop only if they are traveling in the same direction as you on a two-way street.

B. Pull over and stop if they are traveling in either direction on a two-way street.

C. Pull over and stop if they are on the opposite side of you on a divided highway.

The correct answer is B. If you are driving on a two-way street and you see an emergency vehicle using their siren and lights coming from either direction, you must pull over to the shoulder of the road and stop to give them room to get through.

Question 35: If the car ahead of you is stopped at a crosswalk, you should:

A. Slowly pass the vehicle on the left.

B. Never pass a vehicle that is stopped at a crosswalk.

C. Honk your horn so that they get out of your way.

The correct answer is B. You should never pass a vehicle that is stopped at a crosswalk. Someone could be crossing the street that you are not able to see.

Question 36: If you come to an intersection with a 4-way stop, that means:

A. All cars must stop at the intersection.

B. Only cars traveling east or west must stop at the intersection.

C. Only cars traveling north or south must stop at the intersection.

The correct answer is A. If you come to an intersection with a 4-way stop, that means all cars must stop at the intersection.

Question 37: If you are involved in a collision, you must inform the California DMV within _____ regardless of whether anyone was hurt or not.

A. 5 days

B. 10 days

C. 30 days

The correct answer is B. If you are involved in a collision, you (or someone on your behalf) must information the California DMV within ten days of the event.

Question 38: California considers people to be "*negligent drivers*" if they get the following number of points on their driving record:

A. 4 points in 1 year.

B. 6 points in 2 years.

C. Either A or B.

The correct answer is C. Drivers who receive 4 points on the record in one year, or 6 points in two years are considered to be "*negligent drivers*" by the State of California.

Question 39: Which of the following statements is true?

A. When you drive in California, you agree to have your breath, blood, or urine tested if you are arrested for a suspected DUI.

B. You are not required to have your breath, blood, or urine tested because of privacy laws.

C. Your driver's license will not be suspended if you refuse to submit to a breath, blood, or urine test.

The correct answer is A. When you drive in California, you agree to have your breath, blood, or urine tested if you are arrested for a suspected DUI.

Question 40: It is illegal to wear headphones _____ while driving.

A. At all.

B. In one ear.

C. In both ears.

The correct answer is C. It is illegal to wear headphones or earplugs in both ears when driving because you cannot hear what is happening around you.

Question 41: When are you allowed to drive in a bike lane?

A. During rush hour traffic, if there are no bicyclists in the bike lane.

B. When you are within 200 feet of a cross street where you plan to turn right.

C. When you want to pass a driver ahead of you who is turning right.

The correct answer is B. You can drive in a bike lane if you are within 200 feet of a cross street where you plan to turn right.

Question 42: If you see a signal person or "flagger" at a road construction site ahead, when should you obey their instructions?

A. Only when you see orange cones on the road ahead.

B.. At all times, unless they conflict with existing signs or signals.

C. At all times, no matter what.

The correct answer is C. If there is a person directing traffic, you should follow their instructions at all times, even if they conflict with existing signs or signals.

Question 43: When are you legally allowed to block an intersection?

A. When you entered the intersection on the green light.

B. During rush hour traffic.

C. Under no circumstances.

The correct answer is C. It is always illegal to block an intersection.

Question 44: When approaching a roundabout or traffic circle, you should always:

A. Yield to pedestrians or cyclists crossing the road.

B. Yield to any vehicles that are already in the circle.

C. Both A and B.

The correct answer is C. When approaching a roundabout or traffic circle, you should yield to any pedestrians or cyclists crossing the road.

You should also yield to any vehicles that are already in the roundabout before entering.

Question 45: It is illegal to park your vehicle:

A. In an unmarked crosswalk.

B. Within three feet of a private driveway.

C. In a bike lane.

The correct answer is A. It is illegal to park your vehicle in an unmarked crosswalk.

Question 46: When driving behind a motorcycle, you should keep a _____ second following distance between them and you.

A. 1

B. 2

C. 4

The correct answer is C. When driving behind a motorcycle, you should keep a 4-second following distance.

This way, if the motorcycle stops suddenly or skids, you have a better chance of avoiding a collision.

You did it!

Time to tally up your score.

If you answered at least 38 of the questions correctly, then you passed!

If you did not get a passing score, there's no need to panic. Simply review the questions that you missed and read the explanations again.

This will help you remember the concepts when it comes time to take your permit exam.

PASS the Permit Test with Our Proven Study Guide

If you are looking for an easy-to-read study guide that will help you PASS the permit test, I highly recommend checking out our California DMV Handbook Cheat Sheet.

Our study guide summaries the MOST important and ***commonly tested*** information from the official California DMV Handbook.

You can get the "cheat sheet" on our website at **www.DMVstudy.com.**

Unlike the official handbook which is difficult to read and understand, our "cheat sheet" breaks the information that you need to know for the test into small, bite-sized chunks that are easy to understand and memorize.

Go to www.DMVstudy.com and get your copy today or find us on Amazon.

Made in the USA
Las Vegas, NV
21 May 2022